LIVE SPICE!

UNOFFICIAL AND UNAUTHORISED

LIVE SPICE!

OMNIBUS PRESS

The Spice Girls - Geri, Emma, Mel B, Victoria and Mel C - have done it again! By setting out on their very first world tour, they've put their very long and highly polished fingernails up to those Doubting Thomases who reckoned the feisty five couldn't sing a note. As you read these words, their sizzling two-hour show is storming its way across the globe, leaving all the criticism and tabloid speculation on the Spices' future in its wake and proving that Girl Power still rules. So what is life really, really like for the famous five, spending months on the road performing for you, their fans? Read on and (with apologies to Geri!) all will be revealed!

So after you've read the books, listened to the music, seen the film, worn the body-spray, taken the Polaroid pics, chomped the crisps and toyed with the dolls and the pencil case, isn't it about time you actually saw the Spice Girls play live? After all, aren't they supposed to be a pop group? And isn't that what pop groups do - spend half their life in a tour bus going from one city to the next, living out of a suitcase?

Well, not quite. It's a measure of the sheer power behind the Spice Girls phenomenon that the Queens of Pop didn't play by the established rules and go on tour after releasing their first album as most groups do. Instead, they did the Girl Power thing, threw away the rule-book and wrote their very own. As they say themselves, "Rules are made for breaking." If there's one thing the Spice Girls cannot be accused of, it's following the pack. After all, it's unheard-of in the pop industry for a group to have notched up worldwide album sales of 36 million without ever playing a live tour. Few, too, have gone platinum in 33 countries at least twice, sold ten million singles worldwide, been photographed with royalty and world leaders and produced a film that broke box-office records - all in under 18 months! Achievements like that would be amazing for any group - but for one that's never done a UK tour, let alone a world tour, it's utterly unbelievable.

As 1997 closed, then, the press were happily re-painting Spiceworld in very gloomy colours indeed; over-exposure, they said, had finally caused the downfall of the raunchiest and mouthiest girls in pop. All the evidence was there, according to the papers - sluggish sales of their second album, getting booed in Spain and the dramatic ousting of manager Simon Fuller. Rumours were rife that the girls were about to split, but nothing could have been further from the truth. "No matter what the papers say, the fans can see through it and support us no matter what," said an unruffled Geri.

Though the fabulous five had teased and tantalised with snippets of their live act - on David Letterman's US TV show, at the Cannes Film Festival and in various appearances on the National Lottery and *Top Of The Pops* - critics had accused them of not being able to sing, citing their reluctance to perform live as proof of their allegations. As rivals came over the horizon in the shapely form of All Saints, the Spice Girls' Girl Power ethic was increasingly being denounced as a huge marketing slogan. And, as Spice Girl dolls vied with the Teletubbies as the most sought-after Christmas gift in the grotto, claims could be heard that the girls themselves were nothing more than life-size plastic pop icons.

The girls were, in reality, stronger than ever - all five united in their plans to put on the most spectacular world tour of the century. A statement on their decision to take the managerial reins simply said: "We felt in our hearts this is the right decision for us. We would like our fans to know we are positive and excited about the future!" Girl Power was clearly as strong as ever, the Girls insisting "We'll show all our fans we are still the best."

And that's exactly what they've done with the 'Spiceworld Tour', which will see them play over 80 dates in several countries throughout the course of 1998. The five most famous women in pop won't be seeing much of their home and family during this most exciting of years - in fact, the papers have even claimed they're going to be tax exiles! But don't worry: rumours that they're about to set up home in another country have been wildly exaggerated. Besides, there's absolutely no way they're touring for the cash: taking a spectacular show like theirs on the road across three different continents is a massive undertaking and certainly not cheap.

What's more, of course, life on tour - living out of suitcases, constant shows and rehearsals without a day off and being away from loved ones - is nothing short of gruelling. "Obviously you miss family and friends," admits Victoria, doubtless with a certain Mr Beckham in mind, "but there's always the phone. I miss things like British TV - even though I don't watch it a lot of it! I miss British magazines too - whenever we're home, we stock up on them."

Emma simply says she misses her mum! "But at the end of the day," she adds, "I'm with four of my best mates and we always have a laugh. At the moment, I think we're stronger than ever!"

The Spice Girls decided to do the tour not to prove their critics wrong - after all, they know they can sing live - but for the many millions worldwide who've bought their records and turned them into the superstars they are. "We know it will be great," Mel B announced firmly as the opening night approached. "We don't have to prove anything to anyone but ourselves and the fans." Mel C agreed: "To be honest, we're doing this for the fans more than anything else."

The fab five were obviously highly excited at the prospect. According to Scary Spice, other commitments have been the main reason why the Girls had yet to do a tour - not because they didn't have the bottle. "We've been desperate to do a tour in the UK since 1996," revealed the lass from Leeds, "but there were so many other things we had to do first. But now we're really looking forward to the tour." Simon Fuller, still at the managerial helm at this point, confirmed her statement by saying: "Plans for a world tour are set in stone." And what a tour it promised to be.

Though the two shows in Dublin in February of this year that kicked off the 'Spiceworld Tour' were seen as the real test, and attended by almost as many pressmen as Spice Girls fans, the group's live baptism of fire had taken place the previous October in a very unlikely location. The event was held at the Abdi Ipekci, a basketball stadium in the Turkish capital of Istanbul and was attended by worldwide winners of a competition sponsored by Pepsi - one of the Girls' major endorsements. It's doubtless no coincidence that Turkey is apparently the only European country where Pepsi outsells Coke!

If the fans were at fever pitch, then the temperature at the stadium climbed even higher when, as they performed 'Naked', the Girls threw off their black cloaks in dramatic and provocative fashion. The girls had indeed pulled it off - if not stripped off! - and both concerts were judged a roaring success. The next day's headlines spelled out the triumph in sky-high type: from 'Fab Five Turk 'Em By Storm!' (*The Sun*) through 'Istanbrill' (*The Star*) to 'It's Good To Turk' (*The Mirror*), the Girls were the talk of the tabloids.

Since taking Turkey by storm, the Spices had found their time taken up jetting about the planet doing promotional work for *Spiceworld The Movie*, due out on Boxing Day, and the second album of the same name which preceded it.

To the evident delight of their Turkish audience, the feisty fivesome played two shows in front of a magnificent set built like a huge rollercoaster, a glitter-sprayed Mini motor car being poised at each of the peaks. A huge video screen filled the back of the stage so the fans could see close-ups of their favourite Spice Girl, thanks to a team of hydraulically controlled cameras that zoomed around them like hawks about to pounce. "There's going to be a massive party vibe," Geri had predicted - and she was absolutely right! From the moment the gig kicked off with the double dynamite pairing of 'If U Can't Dance' and 'Who Do You Think You Are' the audience was up on its feet as the girls gave an energetic and polished performance.

After spending Christmas with their families, they were whisked away to a a secret location in Ireland to practise for their upcoming tour - a globetrotting extravaganza of gigs spanning three continents and too many counties to mention." The Pepsi concert was almost like an appetiser," announced Geri. "The main course starts in the New Year."

Though they wanted to keep the contents of the show under wraps, they revealed a few tit-bits to their fans in inimitable style. "There is one rude bit in the show," said Geri mysteriously, while Mel B talked about "Lots of different scenes and all different kinds of music - reggae, pop, jungle, hard house and ballads."

The show was set to be nothing less than a multi-cultural event, the Girls promising numerous costume changes along with a ballet routine and dances from around the globe. "We've travelled around the world and picked up a lot of the cultures and learnt a lot," explained Emma, "so we came back with that to write the album (*Spiceworld*)." The show promised to be every bit as eclectic, while Mel C emphasised its all-action style: "It will be extremely physical so we're going to get very fit."

Rehearsal time was strictly limited since, as Mel B explained, "We had to cram everything in because we were in America to promote the movie. We've just been so busy." All went well, though, as the Scary one smilingly explained. "Everyone's buzzin' after the rehearsals and the shows will be full of surprises, very similar to the Madonna show!" Comparing yourself to the Material Girl, who'd been performing live since the early 1980s, certainly showed no lack of confidence.

Three short weeks of rehearsal simply shot by, and before they knew it the big night had arrived. On 24 February 1998 the Spice Girls were about to face the biggest test of their pop careers. On the morning of the first of two shows in Ireland at Dublin's legendary Point Depot, Mel C admitted that she was "scared to death" at the prospect of their first major concert in front of 6,000 fans. If truth be told, they were all feeling the pressure.

"We are excited and nervous!" admitted Emma. "Having your best friends around makes things a lot easier, but the first night is going to be pretty nerve-racking - we don't want to fall over on stage or anything!". All five had devised their own ways of coping before a big live gig, and always come together to perform the Spice Girls ritual before going onstage. "We all have a rugby scrum and shout, 'C'mon!' reveals Mel C. "You know the way Madonna says a prayer before she goes on stage? Well, we don't pray, we just swear and jump about a lot - that gets us all psyched up."

In true Girl Power style, they even insisted the DJs who warmed the crowd up must be female. As Liverpool lass Mel C explained, "We wanted girls because that's what we're all about. We've picked them from the towns and cities we're singing in to make it more regional as well." The hand-picked backing musicians whose task it was to recreate the hits on stage were a talented bunch of professionals whose previous employers had included big names like Massive Attack and Simply Red.

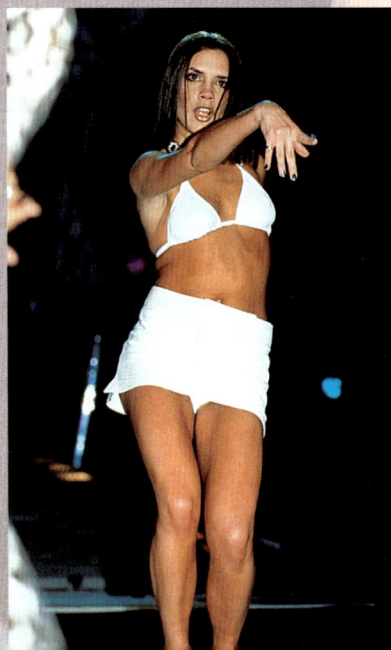

As the world waited to see how the five would react to their biggest challenge yet, one special lady watching from the sidelines had no doubt they would cope perfectly well. She was vocal coach Pepi Lemer, who had given all five singing tuition earlier in their career. "I know they can sing live," she said proudly, "because I've trained them to. I watched them do it at their showcase (their record-label audition), and they did it very, very well. They breathed together, they sang together, they were absolutely brilliant."

As far as the Girls themselves were concerned, their fans were their number one priority. And, as the scrabble began for tickets for the 20-date UK leg of the tour, they made sure those fans would get first shot at taking their place in the audience by making tickets initially available only to people on the Spice Girls database and subscribers to their official *Spice* magazine. "We want to make sure people who come to our concerts are real fans," explained Geri.

As ever, though, the Girls had learned what to do and then adapted it in their own special, Spicy way. For instance, we strongly suspect one particular aspect of their pre-concert preparation might not have come from Ms Lemer's instruction booklet. When Mel B was asked how she protected her voice before a show, she revealed, "I drink a lot of brandy!"

When the Spice Girls had first announced the forthcoming world tour, the demand was phenomenal - as it is for anything with the Spice label on it. Applications for tickets easily outstripped supply and they were snapped up within hours, leaving many disappointed. This all proved that cynicism in the press about the girls' ability to sing live was ill-founded, and utterly disproved a survey by BBC's Here And Now programme which claimed 68 per cent of Spice Girls fans said they wouldn't want to hear them play live.

It's interesting that the Girls decided to play the opening night in Ireland at the famous Point Depot, Boyzone's local stamping ground. Many a big band has played here over the years, though it's a venue most acts take several years to work up to filling. By putting it first on their list, the Girls showed they had confidence a-plenty and that tabloid sniping about the extent of their talents was well out of order.

The Point's 6,000 capacity sold out within two hours and touts were doing a roaring trade outside the venue with tickets going for up to an alleged £150. As Geri, Mel B, Mel C, Emma and Victoria polished up their dance routines and made the final preparations backstage, the queue of fans had already surrounded the famous venue. And then it was time for the show to begin.

As the curtain rose, the audience couldn't fail to be knocked out by the sight of the futuristic stainless-steel set and dazzling lightshow. The music then began, an amazing Star Wars-style countdown booming from the speakers which whipped the crowd into a frenzy. Then came the Girls themselves, who went on to treat the audience to a magnificent show that lasted over two hours. "We will make about six costume changes because we want it to be really theatrical," said Mel B - and the famous five lived up to her words.

After kicking off with 'If U Can't Dance', the crowds went wild as the Girls launched into their mega-hit 'Who Do You Think You Are'. Relaxed and confident, they performed like the real pros they are, even finding time to joke with the audience. At one point, Mel C danced her way centre stage and poked fun at Posh Spice's fiancé, footballer David Beckham: "Cheer if you reckon Liverpool are better than Manchester United!" she yelled with a grin. And as they launched into 'Denying', a standout track from the new second album, the Spice Girls were clearly enjoying every second.

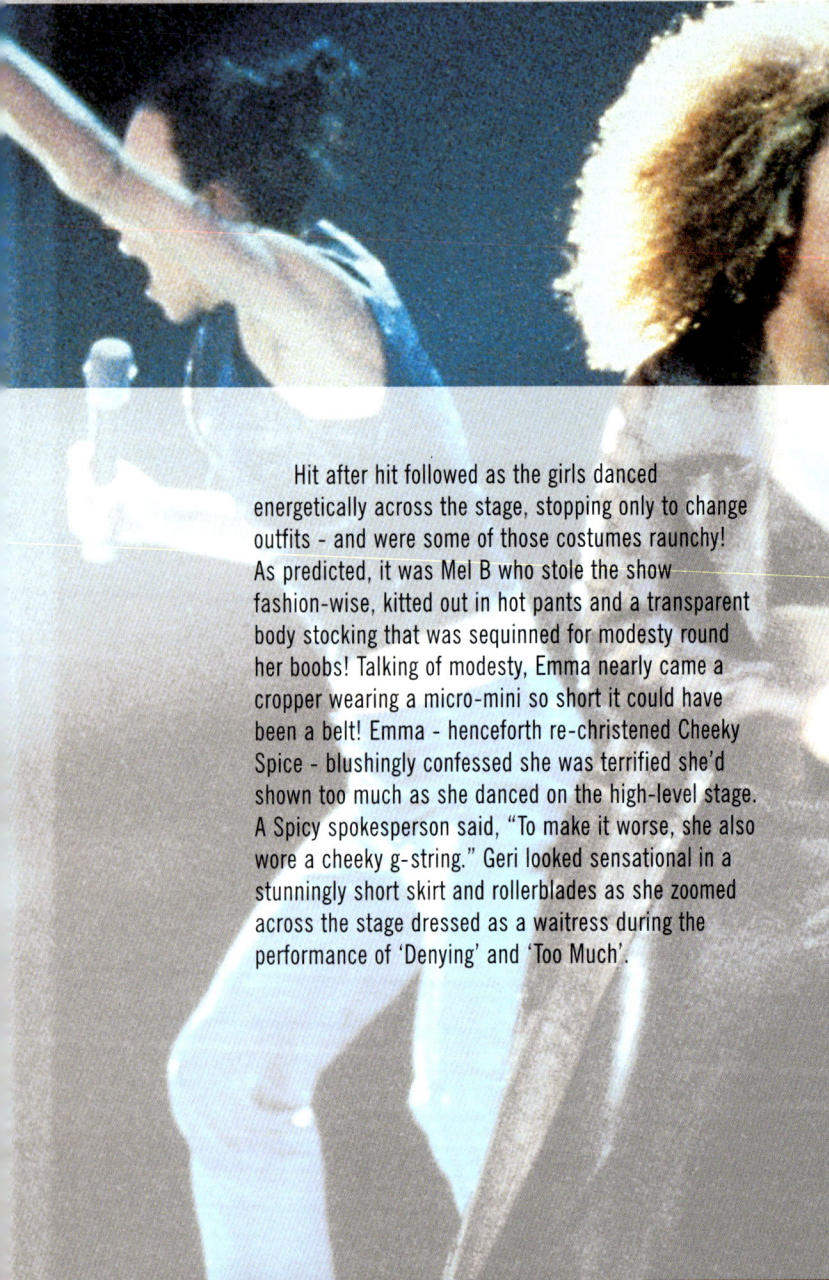

Hit after hit followed as the girls danced energetically across the stage, stopping only to change outfits - and were some of those costumes raunchy! As predicted, it was Mel B who stole the show fashion-wise, kitted out in hot pants and a transparent body stocking that was sequinned for modesty round her boobs! Talking of modesty, Emma nearly came a cropper wearing a micro-mini so short it could have been a belt! Emma - henceforth re-christened Cheeky Spice - blushingly confessed she was terrified she'd shown too much as she danced on the high-level stage. A Spicy spokesperson said, "To make it worse, she also wore a cheeky g-string." Geri looked sensational in a stunningly short skirt and rollerblades as she zoomed across the stage dressed as a waitress during the performance of 'Denying' and 'Too Much'.

The highlight of the show was the appearance of five handsome hunks who joined the Girls for a steamy dance performance. Each 'Spice Boy' had distinguishing features to match their female counterpart: Mel B's had a pierced tongue, Mel C's a tattoo and Geri's had red hair. If you want to know what Baby and Posh Spice's lads looked like, you'll just have to bag yourself a ticket, 'cos we're not giving everything away! The audience, which had played its part in making the Dublin gig a night to remember with a barrage of cheers and screams, were excited to fever pitch when the five muscular males made their surprise entrance. At that point, the feisty five females were strutting about like supermodels on a catwalk while the opening bars to 'Move Over' thundered out behind them.

The Boys, clad in tight-fitting vests and bum-hugging leather pants, writhed and wriggled to the music in an orgy of spectacular showmanship - though, in true Girl Power style, the girls showed the lads who wore the trousers by debagging one poor unfortunate to the delight of the screaming fans! The laydees roved across the stage with a glint in their eyes and only one thing in mind - making mischief. In one stunt, Baby Spice grabbed hold of Scary and gave her a playful nudge off the stage, while Geri and Victoria staged a mock fight before indulging in their Spice Boy striptease act!

The Girls adopted a Supremes-like look as they sang their latest hit single, the Motown-soundalike 'Stop!', appearing in a 1960s-style car and dolled up in 1960s outfits - just as they had in their Brits Award performance two weeks earlier. The Supremes influence was repeated later in the show when Emma took the spotlight and gave a very impressive solo rendition of 'Where Did Our Love Go?'.

Baby Spice proved once and for all that the Spice Girls can sing as she electrified the audience with her powerful delivery of a song that topped the charts for Diana Ross and company long before she was born. Though she'd been a target for the tabloid hacks who criticised her for not excelling in the vocal department, that's not the way the fans saw it!

During 'Naked', the girls donned outfits even more sizzling than the ones they wore for their performance of the track in Turkey. This time, the raunchy Spices wore only flesh-coloured undies, so when they whipped off their top clothes they appeared to have nothing on at all! The carnal cavorting continued as the girls joined together for a raunchy conga to accompany 'Spice Up Your Life' - the Spiceworld album's first single whose live performance all but brought the house down.

Another big highlight of a show that never let up was a powerful duet by the Mels. They joined forces to deliver a superbly soulful version of the Eurythmics' 'Sisters Are Doin' It For Themselves', a song the group could well adopt as their very own anthem. The original hit had paired Annie Lennox with Queen of Soul Aretha Franklin, a class act that would be tough for anyone to follow. But these Spicy sisters were doing it for the fans, who shrieked their appreciation of an unexpected treat.

For the final act, the famous five went all 1970s and kitted themselves out in fabulously funky gear to belt out a dynamic disco duo, 'Never Give Up On The Good Times' segueing into the classic Sister Sledge number 'We Are Family'. Then it was all aboard the Spiceship as they were transported, via the huge video screen behind them, to *Spiceworld*, leaving their ecstatic fans baying for more.

All five girls had put on polished performances, looking sensational in stunning outfits and dramatic make-up. Victoria added her usual note of sophistication in a spangly, figure-hugging cat-suit and tight slinky dresses, sporting her new posh 'Spice Laydee' hair-cut for good measure. Baby Spice lived up to her name in baby-doll dresses, while the ever-irrepressible Geri was busting out all over, showing ample cleavage in her trademark spangled hotpants and bustier-style tops. Not to be outdone, the Mels donned eye-catching bra and crop-tops in hi-glitter Lurex with hip-hugging pants that showed off their stunning figures to the full.

The 'Spiceworld' show had combined state-of-the-art video graphics, slick choreography and a plethora of pop hits belted out with (Girl) power and polish, all of which came together to produce a sensational spectacle. Their vital vocals and dynamic dance act delighted an audience which ranged in age from six to 66, grannies and schoolgirls alike enjoying the experience.

The five had taken their fans on a rollercoaster ride of live music and dance, putting on a truly breathtaking show. Crowds of girls screamed and wept hysterically at the sight of their idols throwing themselves about onstage, while many teenagers were overcome with excitement and had to be tended by waiting St John's Ambulance crews. It was the kind of emotional reaction only a group of the Spice Girls' stature could possibly inspire.

After a show in which the five had obviously given their all yet were still high on adrenalin, it was all back to the hotel, where each Girl had her own way to unwind. "Mel B's room is the party room," the other Mel explained, "whereas mine's the boring one! I'm a real early bird - off down the gym every morning! I love to party, but there's a time and a place for everything, isn't there? I love work, so I like to be fit for it."

Weeks of preparation had gone into the first leg of the tour and all the effort had paid off, so now it was time to get ready for the UK stage. By the time the British leg started in Glasgow on 4 April, the Spice Girls would have neared the 40 million mark in terms of worldwide album sales. By the end, they would hope to have acquitted themselves with the most polished performances of their short but hugely successful careers, proving beyond doubt that they were a live act to be reckoned with.

Next would come dates in Paris, Vienna and Scandinavia before an American tour scheduled to take up June, July and August. And the Spice Girls could face that musical marathon with no fear whatsoever, having managed not only to crack the American market but dominate it. Asia and Australia, two areas where they'd already been taken very much to heart, would follow.

Having survived a storm of press criticism, the highly publicised departure of their manager and supposedly plummeting record sales, they'd come out the other side smelling of roses. The Spice Girls were still the biggest musical phenomenon in the world - not that the fans had needed convincing! You only had to look into the audience waving their banners of appreciation, screaming hysterically with hands outstretched in an effort to reach their idols, to realise that Geri, Emma, Mel B, Victoria and Mel C were still the undisputed Queens of Pop.

And they were determined to enjoy every minute of their reign. "When we're together we have the biggest laugh," says Geri. "It's like being on holiday all the time - we just do work along the way! We've never been better friends, and we call home less than we used to. We know this whole thing could end tomorrow, so we don't take any of it for granted. We're happy with what we've achieved, and we're making sure we all enjoy it while we can!"

"It's gonna be different and it's gonna be Spicy, but you'll just have to wait and see! It'll be a massive party, and I think some people will be shocked!"
EMMA

"I couldn't live in just one place because I do so much travelling. I'll probably get houses all over the world."
VICTORIA

"We've been living out of suitcases for the last two years so touring isn't really that much of a shock to us. But I'm really looking forward to taking a break."
EMMA

"This is our way of giving something back to the fans. Performing is what we enjoy most. We spend a lot of time doing promotion, but you don't get the same kind of feedback as when you're performing live."
VICTORIA

"We have a mad half-hour before a show when we run around, shout, scream, swear and make funny noises. It's like a bonding thing, hahaha!"
EMMA

"When I'm on tour I miss the silly things like Heinz Baked Beans and just nipping down to Sainsburys!"
MEL C

"After a show some of us are so fired up that we can't get to sleep, so we party until we're totally worn out!"
MEL B

"You can't get lonely when there's five of you travelling around together. We have such a giggle, and, even when we work, it's fun. We're always laughing!"
MEL C

"I can't wait for the tour! Letting rip on stage, doing yer thing and just going for it I love that!"
MEL B

"Our plan is for them to follow their own paths but with the support of the each other. I think Geri and Victoria could be actresses, Mel C is the new Annie Lennox, Emma has an amazing pop voice and Mel B is a real soul diva."
EX-MANAGER SIMON FULLER

"When we're nervous and excited we all handle it in different ways. Mel B gets really boisterous, whereas I just sit in the corner and don't speak to anyone!"
MEL C

"It really is a celebration of music. Even if you're not a
Spice Girls fan, we've really tried to make our show entertaining."
GERI

"Our shows are going to be like nothing you've ever seen before!"
MEL B

"I reckon Emma was the most naturally talented -
she had a pretty voice, not a lot of power, but it was there.
The two Mels had a way with soul licks."
VOCAL COACH PEPI LEMER

"Mel B's got truckloads of luggage! She's excessive!"
GERI

"The Spice Girls already had the ambition and wanted success and fame – I didn't teach them that, they had that. They just wanted to know how to get there."
PEPI LEMER

"I think our home is when we're on stage."
MEL C

"It will be brilliant. We expect everyone from little kids to pensioners to have a good time. I'm so proud of us all because we've worked really hard and our voices are sounding good!"

GERI

"We are travelling the world a lot and you know certain little comforts you really appreciate, like when you like your food. We get cross if our food isn't on time, or if the tomato ketchup isn't there."

GERI

"I love all that rock'n'roll partying. I'm sure there'll be loads of wild nights. That's the Spice Girls' philosophy: to have a good time - and we do! Well, having said that, Mel C's always going to bed early!"

GERI

"It's about us enjoying ourselves, getting out there, performing our music."

EMMA

"I think as long as there is a big demand for Spice Girls, we might as well carry on doing it. But as soon as somebody says, 'Oh no', then maybe we'll stop."

MEL B

"This is a fickle world. It's like one minute Take That are the hottest thing, and that's just the way of the 1990s. You over-indulge in everything until the new thing comes along."

GERI

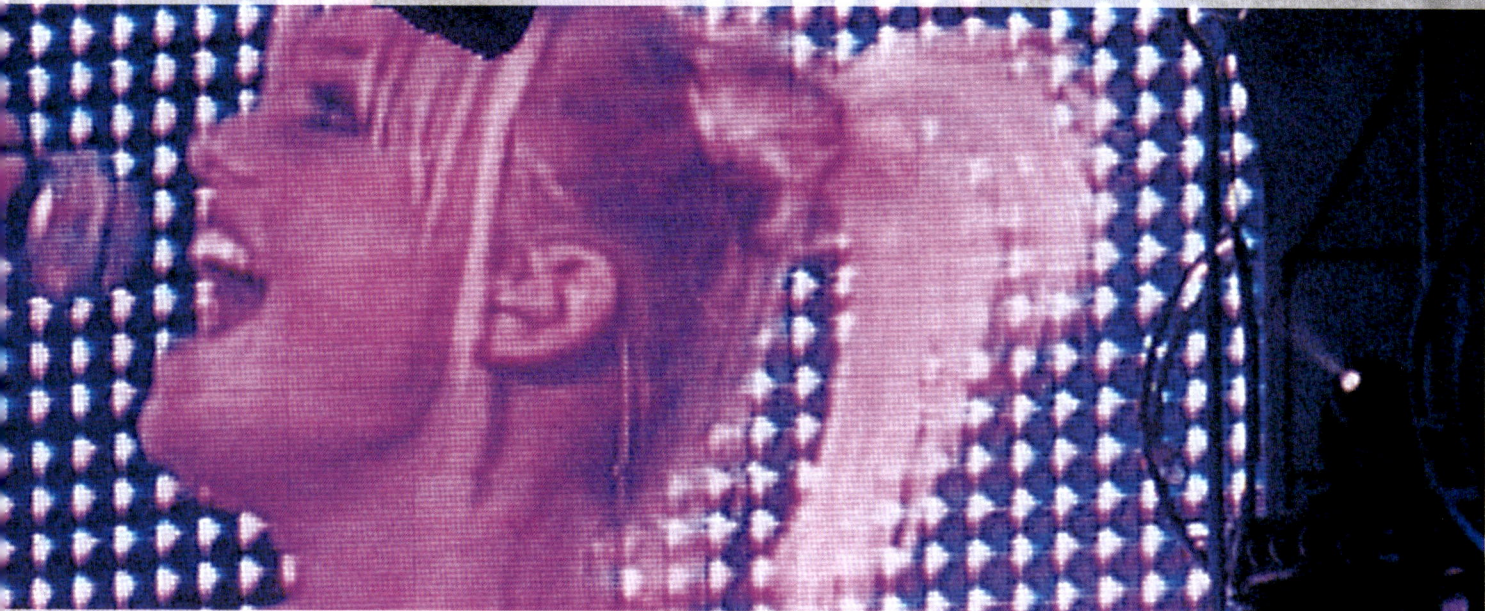

"I never thought I'd get to travel.
Not so long ago it was a big deal for me to go to London.
I ring home now and say, 'I'm in Japan' or
'We're just leaving New York' and it feels so strange as I say it."

MEL C

"I ran out on stage in Japan thinking
the other girls were behind me. I was shouting, 'Hi Tokyo!'
Then I looked around and saw I was totally alone."

GERI

"It's going to be very theatrical - we want to rock!"

MEL C

"I have had singing lessons.
I went to a voice coach and she taught me how to do a bit
of opera which, as you can imagine, didn't quite work
for the way I wanted to sing."
MEL B

"At the moment we're doing rehearsals for our tour and you're
trying your hardest, so sometimes you get angry with yourself."
EMMA

FEBRUARY

TUES 24 WED 25
SPICE GIRLS
SOLD OUT

BOXOUT - TOUR DATES

If you want to know when the Spice Girls will land at a venue near you then check out the full listing of European tour dates below. But unless you've already got a ticket you may be disappointed 'cos the shows are sold out! You could try your luck with the ticket touts if you've got £150 to spare!

24	February	**Dublin Point**
25	February	**Dublin Point**
2	March	**Zurich**
3	March	**Frankfurt**
5	March	**Bologna**
6	March	**Rome**
8	March	**Milan**
9	March	**Milan**
11	March	**Marseille**
14	March	**Barcelona**
16	March	**Madrid**
19	March	**Lyon**
20	March	**Lausanne**
22	March	**Paris**
23	March	**Paris**
26	March	**Munich**
28	March	**Arnhem**
29	March	**Arnhem**
31	March	**Antwerp**
1	April	**Dortmund**
4	April	**Glasgow SECC**
5	April	**Glasgow SECC**
7	April	**Manchester Nynex**
8	April	**Manchester Nynex**
11	April	**Manchester Nynex**
12	April	**Manchester Nynex**
14	April	**London Wembley Arena**
15	April	**London Wembley Arena**
18	April	**London Wembley Arena**
19	April	**London Wembley Arena**
21	April	**London Wembley Arena**
22	April	**London Wembley Arena**
25	April	**London Wembley Arena**
26	April	**London Wembley Arena**
28	April	**Birmingham NEC**
29	April	**Birmingham NEC**
2	May	**Birmingham NEC**
3	May	**Birmingham NEC**
5	May	**Birmingham NEC**
6	May	**Birmingham NEC**
12	May	**Paris**
13	May	**Paris**
15	May	**Vienna**
16	May	**Vienna**
19	May	**Stockholm**
20	May	**Stockholm**
22	May	**Copenhagen**
23	May	**Copenhagen**
25	May	**Helsinki**
26	May	**Helsinki**
28	May	**Oslo**
29	May	**Oslo**

| June, July, August | **America** |
| To be confirmed | **Asia & Australia** |

BOXOUT - THE SPICE GIRLS' SETLIST

If you're one of lucky ones who've got a ticket to one of the forthcoming concerts here's the setlist to whet your appetite. If you're one of the unlucky ones - read it and weep!

IF U CAN'T DANCE ■
WHO DO YOU THINK YOU ARE ■
DO IT ■
DENYING ■
TOO MUCH ■
STOP ■
WHERE DID OUR LOVE GO? ■
(SOLO BY EMMA)
MOVE OVER ■
LADY IS A VAMP ■
SAY YOU'LL BE THERE ■
NAKED ■
2 BECOME 1 ■
WALK OF LIFE ■
SISTERS ARE DOIN' IT FOR THEMSELVES ■
(DUET WITH MEL B AND MEL C)
WANNABE ■
SPICE UP YOUR LIFE ■
MAMA ■

ENCORE:
VIVA FOREVER ■
NEVER GIVE UP ON THE GOOD TIMES ■
WE ARE FAMILY ■

SINGLES

WANNABE
Released July 1996
Highest UK chart position: 1

SAY YOU'LL BE THERE
Released October 1996
Highest UK chart position: 1

2 BECOME 1
Released December 1996
Highest UK chart position: 1

WHO DO YOU THINK YOU ARE/MAMA
Released March 1997
Highest UK chart position: 1

SPICE UP YOUR LIFE
Released October 1997
Highest UK chart position: 1

TOO MUCH
Released December 1997
Highest UK chart position: 1

STOP
Released March 1998
Highest UK chart position: 2

ALBUMS

SPICE
Released November 1996
Highest UK chart position: 1

Wannabe
Say You'll Be There
Love Thing
Last Time Lover
Mama
2 Become 1
Who Do You Think You Are
Something Kinda Funny
Naked
If U Can't Dance

SPICEWORLD
Released November 1997
Highest UK chart position: 1

Spice Up Your Life
Stop
Too Much
Saturday Night Divas
Never Give Up On The Good Times
Move Over
Do It
Denying
Viva Forever
Lady Is A Vamp